MW00721574

FAMILIES OF GOD

Written by
Susan Swanson Swartz

Illustrated by
Deborah A. Kirkeeide

Augsburg
MINNEAPOLIS

FAMILIES OF GOD

Copyright © 1994 Augsburg Fortress

All rights reserved. Except for brief quotations in critical articles or reviews, no part of this book may be reproduced without prior written permission from the publisher. Write to: Permissions, Augsburg Fortress, 426 S. Fifth St., Box 1209, Minneapolis, MN 55440.

ISBN 0-8066-2773-5   LCCN 94-72209

Manufactured in the U.S.A.   AF 9-2773

98   97   96   95   94   1   2   3   4   5   6   7   8   9   10

Families here,
families there.

We're all in God's family
everywhere!

All kinds of families,
all sizes, all faces,

Alone or together
in all kinds of places.

Families here,
families there.

We're all in God's family
everywhere!

On the sea,

near the sand.

By the water,

on the land.

Families here,
families there.

We're all in God's family
everywhere!

Near the mountains,

in the valleys.

In the cities,

near the alleys.

Families here,
families there.

We're all in God's family
everywhere!

Where it is cold,

where it is snowing.

Where it is hot,

where it is blowing.

Families here,
families there.

All kinds of families
in all kinds of places.

God's love shines through
on all of their faces!

Families here, families there.

We're all in God's family everywhere!

Word List

all	family	mountains	the
alleys	God	near	there
alone	God's	of	their
and	here	on	through
blowing	hot	or	together
by	in	places	valleys
cities	is	sand	water
cold	it	sea	we're
everywhere	kinds	shines	where
faces	land	sizes	
families	love	snowing	